A CHURCH THAT SPREADS

ACTS (Part 2)

by Bill Rasco

21st ℰ

ISBN: 978-0-89098-577-9

©2010, 2019 by 21st Century Christian
2809 12th Ave S, Nashville, TN 37204

Unless otherwise noted Scripture quotations are from the New International Version.

Cover design by Jonathan Edelhuber

Table of Contents

Introduction

Evangelism. Now there's a word that has gone out of style. Overbearing sales techniques, one-approach-fits-all methods of sharing the good news have turned a lot of people off. In an adult classroom setting a friend summed up our lack of evangelism as succinctly as I've ever heard, "There are only two reasons we don't evangelize today. Either we don't really believe that people are lost without Jesus Christ or we don't care."

New Testament Christians obviously believed that the world was lost without Christ, and they cared enough to endure any hardships to see that the message was delivered to all who would listen. We love to make great claims concerning our brand of "New Testament Christianity." We follow the patterns laid down in the book of Acts. Do we?

A Church That Spreads examines Acts 13 - 28 and challenges us to follow the pattern. Missionary journeys, new church plants, and sharing Christ with a neighbor were just a part of life in the first century, and the church grew. Re-ignite your passion for the lost and your willingness to be a part of a growing church movement. Make your congregation *A Church That Spreads.*

About the Author

Bill Rasco has been serving as the pulpit minister at the Spring Creek Church of Christ since March 2009. He brings with him a deep background in Christian service and ministry. Bill is a graduate of Southern Christian University, with a degree in Biblical Studies. He served as a pulpit minister, youth minister, and education minister before joining the Spring Creek family. He has written several other studies with 21st Century Christian.

Lesson 1
A Church That Spreads
Acts 13:1-3

Key Verse:

While they were worshiping the Lord and fasting, the Holy Spirit said, "Set apart for me Barnabas and Saul for the work to which I have called them" (Acts 13:2).

WARM UP

The world held its breath. On July 20, 1969, the Apollo 11 mission landed on the moon. Over 450 million people around the world listened to the telecast of this historic event.[1] What they heard forever changed the way that man thinks about limits. Placing his foot on the moon, Neil Armstrong uttered a sentence that still rings in the world's collective memory: "That's one small step for (a) man; one giant leap for mankind."[2] With these few words, the boundaries of humankind were forever changed.

Imagine sitting in your living room, listening to the radio. The impact of the message has stunning implications. Stories from Jules Verne no longer seem so fictional. Bedtime rhymes and stories take

---

1   Alan L. Heil. Voice of America: A History. 2003, ISBN 0-231-12674-3 cited at http://en.wikipedia.org/wiki/Neil_Armstrong#cite_note-52. Accessed on April 12, 2010

2   http://www.snopes.com/quotes/onesmall.asp. Accessed March 19, 2010

on a new reality. Suddenly a vision of far flung outposts and new horizons becomes possible. If a man can walk on the moon, what else is possible?

Now imagine that the church has received a message that has the power to change the boundaries of humanity. In truth, we don't have to imagine. We just have to remember. God has already instilled a vision in His people of a church that shines. A people who surrender their lives to being transformed. A people committed to looking like Jesus. He calls us to a transformation that leaves an imprint on the world.

God wants His church to be a church that spreads. A church that touches the world around us with the love and grace of a risen Savior. A church that ignites a fire in the hearts of those who live around us. Jesus touched lives and pointed the people around Him to kingdom living. He calls us to do the same. The church is meant to live so differently from the world that people see the power of God working in our lives.

Acts 13-28 is a picture of a church that spreads. In the space of only a few decades, the church that began on Pentecost spreads throughout the entire world. The power of God's love and light push back boundaries created by nations, walls built by prejudice and pride, and lines drawn by stubborn hearts and wills. Much like Neil Armstrong, we are riveted to the story of how the Apostle Paul takes the cross of Jesus to places that no one had imagined it going.

The missionary journeys of Paul dominate the last half of the book of Acts. These journeys are God's lessons on how the church spreads. Within each journey, the blueprints of characteristics teach us how to leave an impression in the world. In these journeys we will watch Paul share healing with the hurting. We will hear him speak about the power of the cross to change lives. We will see him go places and interact with people who no one had ever dreamed would hear the call of God. Paul lives with no boundaries. A church that spreads lives with no boundaries. The grocery store clerk needs Jesus. The crossing guard and the teacher at your child's school need Jesus. The guy who cut you off in traffic this morning, the neighbor who never smiles, the greeter at Wal-Mart. They all need Jesus. How will we leave an impression? How will we show them the love, grace, and call of God? How will we be a church that spreads?

WORK OUT

Becoming a Church that Spreads

The launch vehicle for a church that spreads is diagrammed in Acts 13:1-3. Here we see the basic model for how God empowers His people to leave an impression on the world. A church that spreads is shaped by God, makes room for God, and joins in the movement of God.

Shaped by God - Acts 13:1

The church of the first century is a picture of a family saturated with the presence of God. As people come into contact with the message of salvation, they surrender their lives to walking with Jesus. Congregations begin to form in Judea and Samaria. The church in Antioch becomes a place where God's presence is distinctly felt. Luke tells us that prophets and teachers are among those who worship at the Antioch church.

The word *prophet* brings to mind a messenger. He is someone who proclaims God's will among God's people. The word *teacher* paints a different picture. A teacher is one who helps us understand what we hear and learn. The church in Antioch was a place being shaped by God. As God's message goes out among His people, they are learning what to do with that message. The Word of God shapes His people. It transforms them to be something different than they were before. It doesn't matter how long someone has walked in a relationship with God; His Word still shapes us. It shapes our hearts to grieve and rejoice with the things that move the heart of God. God's Word shapes our responses – how we feel about sin, how we react to righteousness, and how we treat others. God's Word shapes our mission, teaching us how to live from day to day as a people who point to Jesus. Our joys are shaped by the reality of God's love. Our hope is shaped by the promise of God's mercy. Our actions are shaped by the power of God's grace.

Today the Word of the Lord speaks to us from the Bible. God's perfect revelation to man is meant to bring more than information into our heads; it is designed to lead us to the transformation of our nature and character. The church of today is still being shaped by God as we give ourselves to the Word of God.

Room for God – Acts 13:2

A church that spreads deliberately makes room for God in their lives. The church in Antioch shows us how to make room for God. The Antioch church was a place of worship. In worship, we pour ourselves out at the feet of God. It is a place where we give God praise and adoration. Worship is a time of sacrifice, a time to deliberately set the things of the world aside to be with God. Worship is one way in which we make room for God. In Antioch, the church participated in fasting. Fasting is a great picture of being empty. In the process of putting aside food, we create an empty place in our physical bodies.

We deny the physical need that represents the physical hold that the world too often has on us. Denying the call of the world opens up room for God in our lives. Fasting and prayer go hand in hand. Prayer is a spiritual connection to God. It is a place where we talk to God about filling our lives with His will, His desire, and His power. Prayer is a place where God moves to provide for our needs and transform our hearts. Prayer invites God to fill our lives with His presence. As the church in Antioch come to worship, they pour their lives out. As they fast, they empty themselves of worldly desire. They deliberately make room for God. As they pray, they invite God to fill their lives and direct their steps.

Like Antioch, the church of today must be deliberate about making room for God. If we want to be a church that spreads, we must be a church that moves within the will of God. God creates opportunities for lives to be touched. God empowers His people to make an impression on others through His love and grace.

Deliberately making room for God in our lives means making the most of the opportunities we have to meet Jesus. Worship, Bible study, prayer, fasting, fellowship, and service are just some of the ways that create space in our lives for God. In these moments we empty ourselves and invite God to fill us with His purpose. The church that spreads deliberately makes room for God to transform them to look like Jesus.

Embracing the Movement of God – Acts 13:3

As the church in Antioch is shaped by God, they gather to worship, fast, and pray. They make room in their lives for God. When the Holy Spirit fills their hearts and chooses Saul and Barnabas, the church must decide how to respond. The decision to be a church that spreads is a decision to embrace the movement of God.

You and I face the same decision today. God is moving in our world. Becoming a church that spreads means honoring the way in which He is the touching hearts and lives. Having been shaped by His Word and living with lives open to Him in worship allows us eyes to see and experience the movement of God around us. The question becomes – will we join Him? God calls His people into the world. There we are to stand as witnesses to His grace, lights that shine for Him, and proclaimers of His peace. Sometimes it feels safer to stay within the walls of our church buildings. But the power of the cross cannot be contained. As you and I are transformed, the Holy Spirit speaks loudly to the world about what God can do in the lives of men. A relationship with Jesus brings peace, joy, forgiveness, and hope. Our transformation becomes a letter written to those who need a Savior. The church of today is sent into the world to share the transforming power of a relationship with Jesus. As we live out a life changed by God, we invite others to experience that same transformation.

COOL DOWN

Leaving an Impression

As Neil Armstrong stepped out of the Apollo 11 Lunar Module, he made the first footprints ever to exist on the moon. These impressions will last "for a million years."[1]

Everyday, you and I walk in the world. Everyday you and I leave an impression on the people around us. What is that impression? Is the world seeing how God transforms lives? Are we walking in the world

---

1   http://www.nasa.gov/audience/forstudents/k-4/home/F_Apollo_11.html. Accessed March 19, 2010

as vessels full of the presence of God? Have we embraced the movement of God by sharing His invitation to walk with Jesus in all that say and do?

God calls His church to leave an indelible mark on the heart of the world in which we live. A church that spreads commits itself to being shaped by God. His Word permeates our thinking, choices, actions, and interactions with others, influencing the way we walk in our world. Worship comes to define the spaces of our hearts and the place where we meet God. Opening our eyes to His movement in the world calls us out of our comfort zones, opening doors for lives to be changed by the power of the cross. Christians walk through the world leaving the footprints of Jesus behind. For a church that spreads, these impressions will last through eternity.

Discussion Questions

1. Name five ways in which the Word of God shapes our lives.
2. Why is it necessary to approach Bible study with an eye toward transformation, not just gathering information?
3. How does worship help you make room for God?
4. How are you making room for God in your life every day? How does Colossians 3:1-17 help you to make a plan for being clothed in Christ?
5. How do we learn to open our eyes and hearts to the movement of God around us?
6. What opportunities to spread the example of Jesus do you see in the people around you? How can we embrace the movement of God in these places?

Lesson 2
A Church That Sends
Acts 13:1-48

Key Verse:

The two of them, sent on their way by the Holy Spirit, went down to Seleucia and sailed from there to Cyprus (Acts 13:4).

WARM UP

In 1972, President Richard Nixon made an historic visit to the People's Republic of China. Meeting with Chinese Chairman Mao Zedong, the two leaders began the process of laying the groundwork for peace between the two nations. It was a time in which Americans were worried about the influence of communism. No one wanted to allow any sort of communist thought to gain a foothold on American soil. But Nixon's well-known anti-communist beliefs allowed the American people to trust his motivation for going to China. Nixon would never give in to communist philosophy or accept communist action in the United States. Nixon would uphold freedom and promote democracy. In 1979, a full diplomatic mission was sent to China to build on the groundwork laid by Nixon.[1] Years of hostility and mistrust had been

---

1   http://www.pbs.org/wgbh/amex/china/peopleevents/pande01.html. Accessed on March 19, 2010.

put to rest. In 1977, Democratic Congressman Tom Foley stated, "It took a Nixon to go to China."[2]

Today Christians are sent into the world to lift up Jesus. The world, however, is a scary place. How can Christians walk in the world and be God's people? God empowers His church to live by the standard of Jesus. God expects us to be ambassadors who call the world to peace through the blood of Christ. Reconciliation with God is accomplished as men and women come to know Jesus through the lives of His people. God sends Christians into the world to call the world to Jesus. It takes a sent church to proclaim the love of God in a hurting world.

---

2   http://en.wikipedia.org/wiki/Nixon_goes_to_China_(phrase). Accessed on March 19, 2010.

WORK OUT

"Sent" People - Acts 13:1-5

Being sent is woven into the essence of being a Christian. We live as a sent people. Jesus was sent by God to redeem us and live as God With Us. We are sent into the world as reflections of His image. We are told to go and spread a message. We are sent to shine as lights in a dark world. Being sent implies that we live under someone else's guidance and control. It means that we walk with a divine purpose in a world that is no longer our home.

A church that spreads is a church that realizes God is moving in the world and opens itself up to be God's tool in that movement. His transforming work can best be seen in those people who share a relationship with Him. All Christians live as a "sent" people. Each one is sent into the world to lift up Jesus. Being sent means:

We live under God's authority.

The church in Antioch surrenders itself to the authority of God. Through prayer, study, worship, and fasting, the church in Antioch places itself under God's control. In verse 3, the Holy Spirit speaks and the church listens. Saul and Barnabas are set apart to do the work that God calls them to do. Part of their surrender includes a journey to lift up Jesus. This marks the beginning of what we call the First Missionary Journey.

One of the best pictures of authority is the parent-child relationship. Parents have authority over children. This authority is meant to be used to teach children what is best for them. Teaching children how to act, how to make good decisions, and how to live with others are part of a parent's responsibility. Children are responsible for living obediently in relation to their parents. We know that God, as the creator of man and the Father of His children, has the ability to govern our lives. Recognizing that authority places us in a position of obedience. We obey God because we know that God is able to see and do what is best for us. Living under authority acknowledges that God is moving in the best interests of His people. Being sent means responding in obedience to what is best for us. God wants to transform us. Part of that transformation is learning to live life under the authority of God. We go where He sends. We live as He desires. His will becomes our will. Living under authority teaches our hearts to beat in time with the Father's heart.

We move by the power of God.

Saul and Barnabas are sent to Cyprus. They no longer choose their own direction, but follow the leading of the Holy Spirit. They move at the command of God. Their time, living arrangements, and location are all directed by the will of God. They do not rely on their own power to accomplish their mission, but rather trust in God's power to lead them and protect them.

Power is the ability or strength necessary to accomplish a task. Living under the power of God means letting go of control. Too many times we want to control our environment, our situation, and even the response of those around us. God calls for His people to let go of personal desire and follow the lead of God. His power breaks down the barriers that bar our way. His power pierces hearts, allowing them to be touched by grace. His power calls for us to submit to His authority. God is the One with the power to change lives. We are a living result of that power. The world needs to see a church that walks and trusts in the power of God.

We follow God's vision.

At Salamis, Paul and Barnabas begin to proclaim the word of God. It is God's vision that every person hear the message of Jesus. As a sent people, we are called to lift up Jesus wherever we go.

Whether it is a present reality or a future happening, vision tells us what someone sees. In Romans 8:28-29, we are told that God is working out His purpose in our lives. That purpose is to make us *"conformed to the likeness of his Son."* God's has a vision for all of us. He looks at the world and longs for all men to look like Jesus. In order to embrace God's vision we must first surrender ourselves to looking like Jesus. We must give ourselves over to God to be transformed. Our transformation calls us to live out the likeness of Jesus for the world to see and hear. We lift up Jesus in the world, so that the world may see Him and be drawn to Him.

Barriers - Acts 13:6-12

The Holy Spirit leads Paul and Barnabas to the city of Paphos on the island of Cyprus. While there, they are invited to meet with Sergius Paulus, the proconsul of the area. Sergius Paulus has a desire to hear about Jesus. As Paul talks about the good news of Jesus, the missionary team encounters a barrier in the person of Elymas. Elymas tries to persuade Sergius Paulus to turn away from faith in Christ. This barrier does not stop Paul and Barnabas from living out the definition of what it means to be sent. Rather than shying away from the Jewish sorcerer, Paul holds up the true **authority** of God's Word and calls both the sorcerer and the proconsul to a life of surrender with Christ as Lord. Paul moves in God's **power** to show the proconsul the truth of Elymas' claim. Just as Elymas is hiding the truth – God hides sight from Elymas. The proconsul sees the truth of God's power and believes. He has heard the message and sees the way that God wants to work in his life. He surrenders to God's **vision**.

Like Paul and Barnabas, we walk in a world that encourages us to live by a standard other than Jesus. It may be the standard of wealth, influence, or education. In reality, each of these standards really point to living for self. Living in our own strength. Being a sent people means we will face the barriers of the world with the authority, power, and vision of God. We will surrender over and over to being His people. We will not allow the world to define who we are or what we believe.

Committed to Being Sent - Acts 13:38-48

The end of Acts 13 cements the three characteristics of a sent person. In Pisidian Antioch we see Paul and Barnabas, once again, relying on the authority, power, and vision of God.

1. In verse 38, we see the **power** of God to forgive sins.
2. In verse 39, Paul lifts up Jesus as the **authority** for life and godliness. The Law of Moses is no longer the authority – we live under the authority of Christ.

3. In verses 42-43, the people see Jesus in Paul and Barnabas. They seek to be taught more about Jesus because Paul and Barnabas hold up Jesus in front of them over and over. The people catch the **vision** of God.

COOL DOWN

Ambassadors for Christ

Nixon went to China to bring reconciliation between estranged nations. Christians are sent to show the world that God seeks to reconcile man with Himself. In 2 Corinthians 5:20, Paul names us ambassadors for Christ. Being sent means taking the love of God and the healing power of the blood of Jesus into the world around us. It means living with the conviction that God is in charge, willing and able to transform man, and desires for all men to live in relationship with Him. A church that spreads understands that it is a church that is sent.

Discussion Questions

1. Define *authority*. How do we learn to live fully under the authority of God?

2. Define *power*. How do we learn to depend fully on the power of God in our lives?

3. Define *vision*. How do we learn to embrace God's vision for ourselves? For the world?

4. Read John 20:21. In what way are we called to live as a sent people today?

5. Do we live as a sent people?
   - Do you let the authority of God touch and shape every aspect of your life?
   - Do you move in the power of God or rely on your own strength?
   - Who defines the vision and focus for your life?

6. How will you live as someone sent into your community this week?

7. How does being a church that sends help us to be a church that spreads?

Key Verse:

He listened to Paul as he was speaking. Paul looked directly at him, saw that he had faith to be healed... **(Acts 14:9).**

WARM UP

Spend time in the car with a toddler and you will get a thorough lesson in awareness. They see *everything*! Cars, trees, construction vehicles, dogs, squirrels, everything. Not only do they see everything on the road, everything they see is a "wow" moment. The eighth school bus gets the same "wow" as the first one. With wide-eyed wonder the planes in the sky cause a little finger to point and a little face to get pushed up against the window in excitement, every time. The sense of wonder and the ability to see make a toddler a great teacher.

Awareness is a vital trait of a church that spreads. Awareness is the deliberate act of seeing. What we see can be an invitation to follow God's movement or join Him in an opportunity to lift up Jesus. What we see can be a warning about danger to come. What we see can touch our hearts and move us to compassion. How we see is important. Seeing is the deliberate act of focusing our eyes and hearts on the movement of God around us. A church that spreads is a church that sees.

WORK OUT

Seeing the Father - Acts 14:1-20

Having surrendered to God's authority, Paul and Barnabas continue on the First Missionary Journey. In Acts 14, we see the second half of this journey as they travel through Iconium (Acts 14:1-7), Lystra (Acts 14:8-20), and Derbe (Acts 14:20-21). The return trip includes Attalia (Acts 14:25), and Antioch (Acts 14:26). During this part of their travels, Paul and Barnabas highlight an awareness of God's movement and power. Their vision helps train our eyes to see.

In Iconium and Lystra, the movement of God is abundantly evident.

- **Acts 14:1** - A great number of Jews and Gentiles believe.
- **Acts 14:3** - God empowers Paul and Barnabas to speak boldly for the Lord.
- **Acts 14:3** - God enables them to do miraculous signs and wonders.
- **Acts 14:6** - God protects His servants from harm.
- **Acts 14:9** - God allows Paul to see the faith of the crippled man in Lystra.
- **Acts 14:10** - God heals the crippled man.
- **Acts 14:14-18** - We can see how God has moved in the lives of Paul and Barnabas in the way that they respond in humility and grief at the townspeople's actions.

- **Acts 14:20** – We see God in the hearts of the disciples gathered around Paul outside the city.
- **Acts 14:20** - God protects Paul and spares his life.

A church that spreads is a church that keeps its eyes on God. Our focus is our Lord. With open eyes, we walk through every day and look for the movement of God. We fix our focus on the cross and watch for the ways that God's love intersects with our lives. We watch for how His power moves to bless us and draw us closer to Himself.

Learning to see God's movement is at the root of our faith. We serve a risen and living Lord. In that very belief, we acknowledge that God is moving and active in our lives today. Learning to be a church that sees begins with a commitment to live with open eyes. Most days, we walk through our lives content to focus on the physical. As Christians who have our hope in a world that we have yet to see, it is important that we move our focus from the physical to the spiritual. God makes His presence evident in myriad ways each day. Counting our blessings is a powerful way to begin to see the way God moves in our lives.

Seeing the Adversary - Acts 14:1-20

God's people must be aware of the enemy that seeks to draw us away from the love of God. A church that spreads is going to be a church that must see the adversity brought to bear by our enemy the devil, and the truth about the foe that seeks to sow discord and disharmony around and among us.

The work of the adversary can be clearly seen in Iconium and Lystra.

- **Acts 14:2** - Hard hearts, stirred up the Gentiles, poison their minds against the brothers

- **Acts 14:4** - Division
- **Acts 14:5** - A plot to mistreat and stone God's servants
- **Acts 14:13** - Idol worship
- **Acts 14:19** - The hatred of the Jews of Iconium

Jesus clearly tells us that we have an enemy. We can expect persecution and hardship because of our commitment to live out His nature in this world. Sometimes we will experience the frontal assault of persecution. The snide comments from co-workers. The outrageous claims of television programs about people of faith. At other times, we can see the impact of the adversary's movement in discouragement, complaining, and disagreements among the brothers. Distractions that cloud our vision and make it hard for our hearts to be full of God's love and forgiveness.

It is important that we be a church that remains alert to the movement of the enemy and keeps our eyes open to the truth that Christ has overcome the world. In Ephesians 6, Paul encourages the church to *"put on the full armor of God."* Specifically in Ephesians 6:16, we are told to *"take up the shield of faith, with which you can extinguish all the flaming arrows of the evil one."* Seeing our adversary is the first step in avoiding defeat. God has equipped us to stand firm in His service. Are words of discouragement the arrows of the evil one right now? *"Encourage one another daily, as long as it is called Today"* (Hebrews 3:13.) Are you surrounded by complaining? *"Set your minds on things above, not on earthly things"* (Colossians 3:2). Is there a relationship that is full of disagreements and strife? *"Blessed are the peacemakers, for they will be called sons of God"* (Matthew 5:9). You see? God has a remedy for anything that the devil can throw our way. God has a victory for us to experience. But we must be aware that our enemy is attacking.

Seeing the Lost - Acts 14:1-20

The towns of Iconium and Lystra are filled with people who need to hear the message of the cross and the good news that is found in Jesus Christ.

A church that sees is a church that has eyes for the lost. We must see their faces and their need for Jesus. It is easy to get wrapped up in our own agendas and activities and miss the fact that most of the people we walk by every day need to be touched by His grace and transformed by His love.

A church that sees is a church that actively looks for opportunities to lift up Jesus before its neighbors, coworkers, community, and the world. Looking like Jesus is not just our standard; it means actively living out of His nature and character before the world. Every time you interact with someone, you have the opportunity to shine with the light of Jesus. Every word you speak has the potential of echoing with the voice of God. Your kindness, joy, love, compassion, purity, and integrity point the world to our living Savior, and the grace that is ours as His children.

COOL DOWN

A Church That Sees

Learning to see begins with a commitment to open eyes. Our vision gets clouded by routine, apathy, self-satisfaction, and busyness. Little children open our eyes to the wonder and surprise of the world they are just discovering. God calls us to have the faith and open eyes of a little child. He longs for us to see His hand, shout in wonder at His grace, and watch intently for His movement in the world.

Becoming a church that sees also opens our eyes to the enemy who is seeking to devour us. He wants to devour our peace, our sense of mission, and our hope. Opening our eyes to the realities of the spiritual realm compels us to take a stand in the shadow of the cross. It demands that we fix our eyes on the One who will protect us from the enemy.

Learning to see reminds that God is in charge. It reminds me to look around with the eyes of God, see how He is moving, and the souls He wants to touch with His peace. Seeing God in the world allows me to experience those things that grieve His heart and those things that bring Him joy. Seeing God allows me to surrender to His will and walk at His side. God calls us to be a church that sees.

Discussion Questions

1. How do we learn to be a church that sees?
2. Why is it important for the church to look for the movement of God today? Where do you see God moving in your congregation today? Where do you see Him moving in your life?
3. Why is it important for the church today to be aware that our enemy is active and working against us? How do we learn to be a church that sees the truth about our adversary, the devil?
4. How can your congregation develop eyes to see the lost who surround our homes and church building? How do we open our eyes to the opportunities we are given to lift up Jesus every day?
5. Commit to living with open eyes for God's movement this week. Each day write down one way in which you saw God working in your day. Stop and thank Him for helping you see Him.
6. How does being a church that sees help us to be a church that spreads?

Lesson 4
A Church That Submits
Acts 15:1-21

Key Verse:

After much discussion, Peter got up and addressed them: "Brothers, you know that some time ago God made a choice among you that the Gentiles might hear from my lips the message of the gospel and believe" (Acts 15:7).

WARM UP

In 1969, Frank Sinatra summed up the thinking of a decade when he sang, "I did it my way." The '60s were a time of great change in American culture. The "Greatest Generation" watched as American youth participated in a counter cultural revolution that placed self in the spotlight. The values of the '40s and '50s were replaced with meeting the needs of self. Things like duty and authority took a backseat to self expression and self gratification. The '60s gave way to the "Me Generation" with its emphasis on instant gratification. And it didn't stop there. We now have the "iGENS" – a group defined and shaped by the needs of the individual over the community.

Don't read these words with a sense that "all is lost." Though the world is calling people to focus on self through advertising, music, TV, and legislation, not all have given themselves over to these influences.

People still feel a need to serve. They still have a heart for the hurting. Man still has a fundamental need for God, whether we know it or not. That is why it is so important to be a church that spreads.

Living a life in relationship with God means living for something other than self. Knowing that the world calls us to self can make us aware of our need for Jesus. The first step in walking with Jesus is submission. Submission is the deliberate decision to allow God to direct our steps and guide our path. It requires being willing to let Jesus control our thoughts, decisions, and actions.

A continuing relationship with Jesus requires continued submission. Each day we learn to look more and more like Jesus. Each moment is filled with transformation as we surrender our lives into His hands and are changed by His power. John the Baptizer said it best. *"He must become greater; I must become less"* (John 3:30). A church that spreads is a church that submits.

WORK OUT

Submitting to God - Acts 15:1-6

As the church begins to spread beyond the borders of Israel, Christians share the message of Jesus with the people they meet in their daily lives. As the good news about grace is received openly and warmly by the Gentiles, it creates a backlash among Christians of Jewish heritage. A group of Christians arises from the party of the Pharisees who begin to insist that everyone who comes to Christ must come to Him through the Law of Moses. They demand that circumcision be a requirement for salvation.

Paul and Barnabas return to Jerusalem to participate in the "Jerusalem Conference." It is a pause in the missionary journeys centered around the question of including the Gentiles in the family of faith. It is a time of struggle that calls for submission to God's will.

The way in which the apostles and elders answer this struggle provides a valuable model for the way we must approach the questions that arise in the church today. A church that spreads holds in it a picture of movement. The most important movement of a church that spreads is the move to bow in submission before God.

The Ability of God - Acts 15:7-11

Peter speaks to the crowd and points them to the surpassing *ability of God* to save those who come to Him through Christ. Part of the circumcision issue rises from a belief that the blood of Jesus is not sufficient to bring someone into a relationship with God. Human wisdom says that there must be more and that "more" is the Law of Moses. Peter reminds them of both their inability to save themselves and the complete sufficiency of God to save those who come to Him through Jesus.

We serve a God who is able – able to fulfill all His promises, able to meet all of our needs, and able to answer our deepest struggles. As we grow in Christ, we must learn to submit to God's ability. We tend to want to trust our own ability and depend on our own power and wisdom. When we submit to the exceeding ability of God and the truth that He has the power to touch and reshape every part of our lives and every action, thought, and motivation of His body, the church, we learn to let control rest in His hands. Submitting to the truth that God is able means that we see ourselves in the light of His truth. God is able. God is able to save. God is able to spread His truth. God is able to sanctify. God is able to bring life and growth and spiritual health to

His church. It also means that we understand that we hold no power or special ability of our own. We cannot add any wisdom to God's wisdom. We don't see things that God has somehow missed. We don't believe that our efforts are the power behind transformation.

The Action of God - Acts 15:12

Paul and Barnabas get up and tell the crowd about the way that God has moved among the Gentiles as they heard and received the message of salvation. Paul points to the **action of God**. God opened a door for the salvation of the Gentiles and Paul points the eyes of the Christians in Jerusalem to the marvelous working of God's grace.

As God's people, we are called to watch for and imitate the movement of God. We are to move where God moves. Our actions should mirror the actions of Christ before men. We are called to celebrate and rejoice in the action of God in the lives of men, preparing our hearts for that action each day. The heart of the church must also be ready for the action of God. The action of God will always be directed toward making us more like Jesus. The movement of God in our lives is always transformational, and it is that transformation that He calls us to share with the world. Transformation, however, always requires submission. God decides where, when, how, and what must change in our lives in order to bring us more fully into the image of Christ. We often want to dictate the pattern or rate of transformation both in ourselves and others. Submission calls us to surrender to the action of God in our lives, and His action in us will power the spread of the church.

The Authority of God - Acts 15:13-21

James stands before the people and points them to the **authority of God**. He looks into the written Word of God and points the people to God's plan and vision for all men. He calls the assembly to submit to God's will and allow God's vision to shape their vision.

The authority of God's Word flows from the authority of God Himself. He is sovereign and absolute ruler of our lives. Christ is the head of the church. His Word is our direction. His Word is our standard. His Word is our authority. The Word reveals the character of God, teaching us how to approach God and live in relationship with Him. The Word has the power to train our eyes how to look for God, our ears how to listen to God, our hands how to serve God, and our tongues how to praise God. When we submit to the authority of God, we commit ourselves to walking in His ways and listening to His voice.

COOL DOWN

An Unchanging God

We live in a world that seeks the latest fad or the newest fix. We live in a culture that changes truth almost as often as we change clothes. The world around us tries to formulate its own answers to our questions. How can the church remain true to God in the midst of such moral relativism? The answer is the same today as it has been throughout history. The church must live lives submitted to Jesus.

A church that spreads is a church that submits itself fully to the Lordship of Jesus. Jesus Himself gives specific instructions about how to do that in Luke 9:23.

Deny yourself – Submission requires denial. The world is unable to meet the needs of humanity. The world cannot offer peace that passes understanding, unchanging love, or eternal life. Only by submitting to God can we live the abundant life promised by Jesus. Only

God is able to transform us to be His people.

Take up your cross – God has moved on behalf of all men. The cross is the standard that His people live by. The cross calls us to love beyond reason. To sacrifice beyond self. To live beyond the moment. The cross points to God's action in our lives, and it points our lives to His action in our world. We are a people shaped by the cross, pointing people to God's salvation. Submitting to the cross means we surrender our lives to God's saving grace.

Follow Me – God is in charge. Because of His authority we submit our wills to His. The books we read, the shows we watch, and the music we listen to are all guided by God's will. How we treat others, how we think, and how we feel must be governed by the heart of God. Submitting to God means following the footprints of Jesus in our walk through life.

Discussion Questions

1. To what does Peter point as the answer to the question about the salvation of the Gentiles?
2. To what do Paul and Barnabas point as the answer to the question about the salvation of the Gentiles?
3. What does James point to as the answer to the question about the salvation of the Gentiles?
4. How will focusing on the ability of God, the action of God, and the authority of God help us answer the difficult questions we face as the church today?
5. How does learning to deny ourselves teach us to honor the truth that God is able?
6. How does picking up our cross daily teach us to submit to God's action in our lives?
7. How does Christ's command to "follow me" teach us to submit to God's authority?
8. How does being a church that submits help us to be a church that spreads?

Lesson 5
A Church That Sings
Acts 16:6-34

Key Verse:

About midnight Paul and Silas were praying and singing hymns to God, and the other prisoners were listening to them (Acts 16:25).

WARM UP

Corrie ten Boom, her sister Betsy, and their father were part of a network that moved Jews out of Holland during the Holocaust. Corrie tells her story in her book *The Hiding Place*. It's a story of a family who gave their resources, their home, and eventually their lives to help families escape Nazi persecution. The three ten Booms were eventually captured and spent time in prison, labor camps, and even in concentration camps. In 1944, the barracks at Ravensbruck concentration camp where Corrie ten Boom and her sister, Betsy, were kept were terribly overcrowded and flea-infested.

They had been able to smuggle a Bible into the camp. Reading God's Word together, they learned that in all things they were to give thanks. They heard and believed the promises that God can use anything for good. Corrie's sister Betsy decided that this meant thanking

God for the fleas. This was too much for Corrie, who said she could do no such thing. Betsy insisted, so Corrie gave in and prayed to God, thanking Him even for the fleas.[1]

Over the next several months a wonderful, but curious, thing happened. They found that the guards never entered their barracks. This meant that women were not assaulted. It meant that they were able to do the unthinkable – to hold open Bible studies and prayer meetings in the heart of a Nazi concentration camp. Through this, countless numbers of women encountered the love of Christ.

Only at the end did they discover why the guards had left them alone and would not enter into their barracks. It was because of the fleas.f

A church that spreads rests in the hands of God. No matter where we are or what we face, we know that God's promises are sure. We know that He is watching over us, calling us to be His people in every moment. Circumstances change. Situations alter. But God is a rock, a stronghold, and a refuge that will not move. Because of His great love, we can praise Him in the midst of anything that comes our way. Our hearts can soar in His presence. A church that spreads is a church that sings.

---

1   ten Boom, Corrie. The Hiding Place. New York: Bantam Books. 1974. Pages 197-199

WORK OUT

Meeting God in Community - Acts 16:6-15

Acts 16 marks the beginning of the Second Missionary Journey. God sends Paul and his companions to the region of Macedonia. He carefully directs their steps to soil that He has prepared to receive the seed of the Word. Paul makes his way to the capital city of Macedonia, setting out to find where God is moving in the city of Philippi. On the Sabbath, Paul goes to a place of worship. Philippi has no synagogue, so Paul goes to a place of moving water because he knows that he will meet people there who are looking for the movement of God. (During the time of the Babylonian captivity, Jews who were separated from the temple developed the habit of meeting by places of moving water to worship.) There he meets Lydia and other women of the city who have gathered by the river for prayer. As they worship together, hearts are opened, promises are spoken, and lives are changed.

Worship prepares our hearts to meet God. In worship, we turn our eyes away from ourselves, focusing on the majesty and glory of God. In worship we empty ourselves of self and make room for God to move in our lives. We pour out pride, self-reliance, and the distractions that pull our eyes away, coming before Him with renewed humility, dependence, and focus.

As we prepare to meet God in worship, we open ourselves up more fully to the ways in which God wants to work in us and through us. Our eyes become more aware of His presence. Our ears become more attuned to His voice. Our voices sing and speak His name more readily. Our hands and feet become more committed to His service.

The transformation that takes place as we come together to worship in song, prayer, study, communion, and giving has a powerful impact on both the Christian and the non-Christian as it turns all of our eyes toward God and opens our hearts to His presence.

Meeting God in Adversity - Acts 16:16-25

Sitting in a jail cell in Philippi, Paul and Silas turn to the source of their strength. They commit themselves again to the care of God. They take a time of trouble and determine to rest in the fact that God is present. Hebrews 13:15 names what Paul and Silas are doing a *"sacrifice of praise."* It is a time when they lose themselves in the will of God. Personal discomfort, suffering, and pain are reminders that God is our healer, protector, and provider. A jail cell becomes a place of peace. The clanking of shackles is drowned out by voices lifted in praise.

Worship is an activity that extends far beyond the times of corporate worship that we share together. The heart and mind of worship should touch every moment of our days. We often associate worship with times of overflowing joy and blessing. Worship can also flow from our hearts during times of struggle and great difficulty. Worship powerfully reminds us of who God is and who we are in His care.

Worship reminds us of God's presence.

When we lift our hearts in worship, we move our eyes away from the troubles of the world and seek the face of God. We are reminded of His nearness and His earnest desire to draw us closer to Himself.

Worship reminds us of God's protection.

When the world beats against us and struggles and difficulties make us feel vulnerable and afraid, worship calls our hearts to remember the sovereignty of God. God is in control. The battle rages, but the victory is sure. Not a hair on our head is uncounted and not one of our tears goes unnoticed. He is our fortress and our stronghold, and worship reminds us in whom our strength lies.

Worship reminds us of God's provision.

Worship expresses our confidence in God. He will provide for all of our needs. He will take care of us and bring us safely through life's storms. Worship helps us rest in God's hand and trust His love. It renews our faith and centers our hearts on the sufficiency of His grace.

Meeting God in Praise - Acts 16:26-34

As God moves to protect His servants, His movement prepares the heart of the Philippian jailor to meet Jesus. As the jailor and his family commit their lives to Christ in baptism, overwhelming joy fills their hearts.

Worship is the response of a heart that experiences the presence and grace of God. Praise moves us to exalt God and take our proper place before Him. It opens the way for God to work in our lives to create in us the image of Christ. In worship, we honor His love and the world's pull on our hearts loses some of its power. Worship both fills us up with God's presence, and empties us of the empty things that clutter our lives.

The longer we spend in worship, the more it brings us full circle – it prepares us to meet God in even deeper and more profound ways. We renew our "faith-sight" that reminds us of His protection and provision. It allows us to respond to God with humility and honor as we move deeper into His provision.

As we become a people defined and shaped by worship, the church becomes a place that lifts up Jesus before the world. Transformed lives point to the movement of God. Singing in the midst of difficult circumstances shows the world the true answer to all of life's struggles. Joy speaks to the presence of God in the lives of His children.

Discussion Questions

1. How does gathering by the river for prayer prepare Lydia to meet God?
2. How does worship prepare us to meet God?
3. Read Hebrews 13:15. In what way is Paul and Silas' singing a sacrifice of praise as they sit in prison?
4. How can our worship shine as a light for others?
5. In what way is worship the proper response to God's presence and movement in our lives?
6. Who do you know that you would describe as a person of worship? What have they taught you about Jesus?
7. How will having a heart of worship allow others to see Jesus in you?
8. How does being a church that sings help us to be a church that spreads?

Lesson 6
A Church That Studies
Acts 17:1-15

Key Verse:

Now the Bereans were of more noble character than the Thessalonians, for they received the message with great eagerness and examined the Scriptures every day to see if what Paul said was true (Acts 17:11).

WARM UP

Abraham Lincoln once said, "I believe that the Bible is the best gift God has given to man. All the good from the Savior of the world is communicated to us through the Book." [1]

How true! In the pages of Scripture, you will find a God who pursues mankind with a passion unequaled in any love story. It holds the answers to man's questions. It illuminates the path to eternal life. The Bible is God's perfect revelation to man. It is the story of Jesus and redemption. It is a "lamp to my feet and a light for my path" (Psalm 119:105).

Throughout history, the Bible has been the conscience of kings, the hope of the humble, and offered help for the hurting. But not all

1   Zuck, R. B. (1997). The speaker's quote book : Over 4,500 illustrations and quotations for all occasions (32). Grand Rapids, MI: Kregel Publications.

have held the Bible in high regard. Through the years, many have tried to destroy it. One of the most infamous attempts was by the Roman Emperor Diocletian. In 303 A.D., he issued a decree that called for the burning of all Christian Scripture. He believed that with the eradication of the Bible, Christianity would disappear. The edict was in effect for eight years. Then, in 311 A.D., Galerius, then ruler of the Eastern Empire, issued a decree of tolerance.[2] The persecution withered and failed. Too many were willing to die for faith. Too many were unwilling to give up their study of the Scriptures. Fewer than 20 years later, Constantine took control of the Roman Empire and commissioned Eusebius to provide 50 copies of "the sacred Scriptures…for the instruction of the Church."[3]

What is it about the Bible that inspires such devotion? Why do men and women commit themselves to study day after day for years on end? The answer lies in the fact that people who study are transformed. God speaks through His Word. A church that spreads is a church that studies. A church that studies is a church that roots itself in the Word of God. Studying God's Word helps us see Jesus, helps us become like Jesus, and helps us spread the good news about Jesus.

---

2   Shelley, B. L. (1995). Church history in plain language (Updated 2nd ed.) (94). Dallas, Tex.: Word Pub.
3   Schaff, P. (2000). Vol. 1: The Post-Nicene Fathers (electronic ed.). electronic ed. (0). Garland, TX: Galaxie Software.

WORK OUT

God's Revelation to Man – Acts 17:1-15

Continuing on the Second Missionary Journey, Paul enters both Thessalonica and Berea. As is his custom, he finds a Jewish synagogue.

It is important to see that Paul initially looks for people who have a desire to walk with the Lord, seeking out people who are already familiar with the words of God.

As Paul teaches in the synagogue, he opens the Scriptures and points to Jesus. He helps them see Jesus. In doing so, he demonstrates three important truths about God's Word and its revelation to man.

The Word of God reveals the plan of God.

The Scriptures are the definitive revelation of God's action and interaction with man and for man. In the written word, God shows us His nature and character, calls us into relationship with Himself, and reveals both the sin that blocks our path and the plan that leads us to the cross of Christ. The Word holds up the fullness of God's holiness and provides us with an authoritative standard that teaches us how to walk with God in this world.

Genesis 3:15 holds the first promise of the cross. As man falls into sin, God moves to restore relationship. There would come a day when sin would be crushed and chains of slavery would be broken. That day would find its fulfillment at the cross. What an awesome understanding to know that God has been moving from the beginning of time to draw us into His family. Every move He makes shows us that He is working His will out in our lives. Living with Jesus is no accident. It is the plan of God. Studying the Bible reveals God's plan and how it transforms our lives today.

The Word of God reveals the person of Jesus.

Paul uses the Scriptures we know as the Old Testament to explain and prove that Jesus is the Christ, and to reveal the redemptive work of the Jesus on our behalf. Every word of Scripture ultimately points to Jesus. His birth, life, ministry, and sacrificial death are all painted into the words of the Old Testament.

In Luke 24, two men have an encounter with Jesus. It is the morning of the resurrection and these two men travel the road between Jerusalem and Emmaus. Along the way they encounter Jesus, but do not recognize Him. During the course of their conversation, Jesus tells them what Scripture says about the Messiah. Jesus walks through the Law and the prophets to speak about Himself.

Never forget that Jesus is the central figure of the Bible. God's plan from the beginning of time centers around Jesus and the cross. Each time we enter a study of the Bible we need to look for Jesus shining from the pages.

The Word of God reveals the proclamation we are to share with the world.

As Paul teaches about the gospel, he grounds his message in Scripture. He uses God's own words to point the people to the cross. The bondage of sin, the power of grace, the sacrificial love of a Savior find their fullest expression in the language of Scripture. Paul relies on the authority of Scripture to bring them into an understanding about who Jesus is and how He has moved on their behalf. The Word of God provides us with the same solid foundation today. We must cement everything we say in the firm foundation of God's Word. The message we share with our friends and family is not rooted in the power of our eloquence or the strength of our words. The message of Jesus is grounded in the words of God. We share His promises. We invite people into His embrace. We hold up His power. Studying the Bible helps us know the certainty of God's desire to live with man. That certainty about God's love pours out of our lives into the lives of those we meet every day.

Turning the World Upside Down

As Paul points people to Christ, the transforming power of God's Word becomes evident. Some are drawn to the Redeemer, accepting His invitation to be His. Many receive the Word with joy and eagerness. Others resist the message of grace and even begin to actively work against the spread of the gospel. There are those who open their homes to Paul and his friends, and in doing so put themselves in danger. Others commit to traveling with Paul until he reaches a place of safety.

Acts 17:6 reveals the full impact of the message of the cross – *"These who have turned the world upside down have come here too"* (Acts 17:6 NKJV). Even those who opposed the Word of God recognized the power of its message. It has the power to "turn the world upside down."

God's Word transforms what it touches. When rain and snow fall from heaven, soft soil quickly and eagerly absorbs the life-giving moisture. When it does, it fuels transformation. Fruit is the result of being open to the water God pours out on the ground. In Isaiah 55:10-11, God tells us that His Word works the same way in our hearts. When we allow the life-transforming force of His message to penetrate our lives, it changes us. It shapes us into the image of the Son. When we understand how God wants to work in our lives and the tremendous promise and blessing that each moment spent in study holds, it allows us to approach those moments with nobleness and great eagerness.

In both Thessalonica and Berea, the message of the gospel spread among the people. Some people rejected it violently. Others embraced it with gladness and eagerness. As Paul reasoned with the people from the Scriptures and the Bereans examined the Scriptures daily, the word of God spread. Study provided a platform from which to share the good news about Jesus. When we root our lives in God's Word, it gives us a foundation from which we can proclaim the Christ and showcase the power of the cross. God has already written the story. He calls us to participate in the story, to be changed by the story, and to share the story with others.

Discussion Questions

1. How does Paul help the people see Jesus?
2. Read Luke 24:27 and John 5:39. Why is it important for us to understand that Jesus is the central figure in the Bible?
3. What evidence do you see of the transforming power of God's Word in the lives Paul touches in Thessalonica and Berea?
4. Read Isaiah 55:10-11. Describe the power of God's Word. What promise does God make? How does this promise help us approach the Scriptures with a heart like the Bereans?
5. How does being a church that studies help us to be a church that spreads?

Lesson 7
A Church That Is Single-Minded
Acts 17:16 – 18:17

Key Verse:

God did this so that men would seek him and perhaps reach out for him and find him, though he is not far from each one of us (Acts 17:27).

WARM UP

No matter what the event, Olympic athletes all seem to wear the same look as they compete. From the starting line you can see it, the intense look of concentration. Years of preparation bring focus and clarity. Eyes lock on the finish line. Head and shoulders point toward the goal. There is a single-mindedness that comes with training. An ability to focus on what is most important in the moment. It doesn't matter if the competitor is running, throwing, skiing, skating, riding, or curling. Olympians are single-minded about their goal.

A Single-Minded Objective

Leaving Berea and traveling through Athens and Corinth, Paul takes with him a single-minded objective. First Corinthians 2:1-5 gives us an insight into the heart of Paul. He shares with the Corinthians this thought, *"For I resolved to know nothing while I was with you except Jesus Christ and Him crucified."* In this one statement we see the intensity of Paul's focus. Paul's one desire is to know Jesus. Paul's one standard is Jesus. Paul's one message is about Jesus. Paul resolved, decided, and committed to emptying himself of everything except the cross of Christ.

This kind of resolve sometimes scares us. Words like *fanatic* or *zealot* flash before our eyes. But don't dismiss what God is teaching us in the focus of Paul. If we are going to be a church that spreads, we must be a church that is single-minded. A church resolutely focused on Jesus. The distractions of the world cannot be allowed to pull us away from seeing Jesus. Hardships cannot be allowed to harden our hearts. In every moment, we must be a people defined by the cross.

As we continue to walk through the Second Missionary Journey, Paul teaches us the power and importance of being single-minded about being a disciple of Jesus.

Focus in the Midst of Distraction – Acts 17:16-34

The city of Athens is a crossroads in the ancient world. It is a place where trade goods and travelers, philosophers and ideas all come together to form a culture saturated with different voices – voices that call for the attention of anyone who will listen. It is a place not so different from where we live. Multiple voices vie for our attention. Different morals and ethics swirl in the people and lifestyles that surround us. How do we spread the love of Jesus in today's society? By being a church that is single-minded. By concentrating on one desire, one truth, and one message.

One Desire - Acts 17:16-23

As Paul stands in the midst of the noise that flows through the streets of Athens, he is distressed by what he sees. His heart breaks with the reality that the world and its philosophies have intruded on the relationship between man and God. Everywhere he looks there are idols. Man-made gods draw the eyes and hearts of the people, leading them away from God. But rather than stand defeated or overwhelmed, Paul is single-minded in his desire to lift up Jesus in this community.

It is easy to stand in the midst of our society and not see the idols that permeate our culture. We have lived with them so long; they almost become part of the background. Paul looks at the idols in Athens and grieves over the way that sin has broken the people. He sees their desperate need for God. The idols don't cause him to step away from the culture. Rather they compel him to walk into its midst and begin to talk about Jesus. His heart beats with God's desire to mend the brokenness and call back those who have lost their way. When we look at the world, God wants us to have one desire – to see the devastation of sin made whole by the blood of Jesus. He wants us to resolve to know nothing while we walk in this world except Jesus Christ and Him crucified.

One Truth – Acts 17:24-34

Beginning in the synagogue and working through the marketplace, Paul encounters a variety of people who hold to different beliefs. Yet with every person, Paul talks about Jesus and the resurrection. As Paul lifts up Jesus, more and more people become interested in hearing what he has to say. Some are upset by Paul's preaching. Whether pausing to speak to a vendor in the marketplace or standing in the Areopagus, Paul is single-minded about calling the people to walk with God. He preaches the one truth about the one God and God's one answer for man – Jesus.

Paul talks about God's omnipotence.

God is all-powerful. He is the Creator of the world. He gives life to all men. He is sovereign in the heavens. Because of this sovereignty, He calls man to live in a relationship that acknowledges God as Lord.

Paul talks about God's omniscience.

God knows all, setting the time and places for men to live, so each one might have the best opportunity to come to know Him. He watches over men and knows their every thought, their every action. He is aware of man's need for salvation, and a path to a relationship with God.

Paul talks about God's omnipresence.

God is in every place. If man will just search for Him, man will discover that God is near. God lives within arms reach of man in every moment. He waits for man to simply reach out and find Him.

Paul talks about God bridging the distance between Himself and man through Jesus.

Jesus is proof of all that God is and all that God wants. Through the death of Jesus, the power of sin is demolished by the power of God to forgive. God knows exactly what man needs and fills the need of every man in Jesus. God calls us to see Jesus in every place and every moment and repent – turn away from the voices and pressures of the world and single-mindedly follow Him. In love, God puts our old self to death through the blood of Jesus, raising us to walk as His children in this world.

One Message – Acts 18:1-17

As Paul enters Corinth and begins to share the story of Jesus, he meets resistance from the Jewish population. Abuse, secret plans, and government complaints dog Paul's footsteps. In the face of this hardship, Paul devotes himself to lifting up Jesus. He wants people to see that Jesus is the only answer. That Jesus is the Messiah promised by God for the salvation of the world.

The single-minded call of God must lead to His followers being single-minded. God encourages Paul to continue speaking. God calls for Paul's message to be the very voice of God. Protected and encouraged by the Lord, Paul dedicates himself to being single-minded about lifting up Jesus.

We, too, are called to be single-minded in our focus on lifting up Jesus. Just as Paul was single-minded in every city he visited and with every group he talked to, we must learn to view our world and our opportunities through the person of Jesus.

Jesus must be lifted up in our homes. How we love those closest to us – our parents and children, our siblings and spouse – displays to the world the love we receive from Christ. Our families are a display case for how we have learned to love.

Christ must be lifted up in our work places. The work ethic we display, the integrity we model, the honesty we live by are all markers of how God has transformed our lives. We carry our faith into the marketplace and people take note of our allegiance. People listen to our words and watch our actions. It is a chance to showcase the remarkable work of Jesus.

The Lord must be lifted up in our schools, gas stations, restaurants, and grocery stores. Every word and deed must be a reflection of our focus on Jesus. How we speak to our waitress is a mirror of how we hear God. How we view the clerk or interact with a teacher is a portrait of how God feels about humanity. Every moment must be lived with the single-minded focus that we are lifting up Jesus in our world.

COOL DOWN

Single-Minded

Olympic athletes have one focus. They dedicate their lives, sacrifice time, energy, money, and opportunities, and give themselves completely to a single goal. Paul looked at an athlete's single-mindedness and encouraged us to learn from their example. *"Do you not know that in a race all the runners run, but only one gets the prize? Run in such a way as to get the prize. Everyone who competes in the games goes into strict training. They do it to get a crown that will not last; but we do it to get a crown that will last forever"* (I Corinthians 9:24-25). God gives us one truth to hold up before the world and one message to proclaim – Jesus Christ and Him crucified. He longs for us to be single-minded in lifting up the cross. He wants Jesus to be the one desire of our hearts.

Discussion Questions

1. What is Paul's one desire?
2. What one truth does Paul want to hold up?
3. What one message does Paul dedicate himself to proclaiming?
4. In what way does God call us to be single-minded?
5. In what way is Athens a mirror of our own society?
6. Read I Corinthians 2:2 again. How do we make Paul's resolution our resolution?
7. What impact do you think such a resolution will have on your –
   - Family?
   - Workplace?
   - Church family?
   - Community?
8. How does being a church that is single-minded help us to be a church that spreads?

Lesson 8
A Church That Is See-Through
Acts 19:1-41

Key Verse:

In this way the word of the Lord spread widely and grew in power (Acts 19:20).

WARM UP

On December 29, 2009, Google News ran a report about the development of see-through fish.[1] A group of Japanese researchers have been looking for ways to remove the bad feelings associated with dissecting animals. The see-through fish, bred from goldfish, are the second such animal to be produced. The first was the see-through frog, originally developed in 2007. These animals allow students and researchers to examine the internal workings of the animals as they progress from birth through life. Beating hearts, working lungs, digestive processes are all seen in 3D as the frogs and fish do what frogs and fish do. It is expected to be a breakthrough in education, allowing students to examine life from the inside out.

---

1   http://www.google.com/hostednews/afp/article/ALeqM5gBcxuX2KezA7BF3rlfZjfEdmsv_ A. Accessed May 11, 2010.

See-through frogs give us a whole new way to think about transparency. For the Christian, being transparent means that those around you see Jesus living in you. Transparency gives the viewer a clear focus on what is inside. Like a diamond in a glass case, Jesus is meant to be the treasure shining out of the transparent life of a Christian. The people around us should be able to see how Jesus works in our lives. How our hearts beat in time with His. How our lives are alive with His presence. How we lean on Him in all circumstances. We are called to be a see-through people.

Living see-through lives can be a little scary. In fact, it can be downright intimidating. Just the thought that my life is supposed to resemble the life of Jesus often brings us up short. But God always empowers us to be what He calls us to be. Think for a moment about someone in your life who you would consider to be a "spiritual giant." This is a person who you think about, and then think, "They look like Jesus." This is a person you want to be like when you "grow up." This is a person that is see-through. We look at their relationship with Jesus and want to walk in the same way because we see Jesus shining in them. The way they pray, the way they talk to others, the way they share their faith so naturally is the product of walking with Jesus and becoming transparent in Him.

Now look at your life. In what ways are you transparent? How has Jesus changed your life to shine for Him? Be honest. Don't play the "aww shucks" card. You know, the one where we go, "Aww shucks! I don't look like Jesus. That would be vain to even think that way." If Jesus isn't making a radical difference in our lives, we need to take a look at what it means to be His. The reality is that if we are walking with Jesus, God is working in us so that we can be *conformed to the likeness of His Son*" (Romans 8:29). A church that spreads is a church that is see-through.

WORK OUT

The Focus of a See-through Life – Acts 19:1-12

As Paul begins the Third Missionary Journey, he travels to Antioch, Galatia, and Phrygia to strengthen the disciples. He then travels to Ephesus, where he notices that there is something missing in the lives of the disciples there – the light that shines from Jesus. He asks them a question about the Holy Spirit and baptism. Paul's question goes to the heart of what it means to be see-through - is God living in you? The disciples had listened to the message of John the Baptizer, but had not gone on to hear the voice to which John was pointing. They needed to fully surrender to Jesus and have the Holy Spirit, God living in them. This is the message of Jesus. Paul points them back to the original voice, the voice that contains the power to heal and to save.

Paul's question reveals a stunning truth. God's will is to live inside of His people. He longs to become a part of who we are and how we live. To deny that God is changing us is deny the work of God in our lives. In order to be transparent, we have to be able to see how God is changing us. We have to surrender to His work in our lives. It is not enough to claim to be disciples like the men in Ephesus. People, ourselves included, have to be able to see Jesus shining in us. We have to focus on what God is doing in our lives so that we can show others what He can do in any life.

Paul lives a life of transparency. God works through Paul. The power is God's. Paul lives a surrendered life, and God works through Paul to call men to hear the voice of Jesus. It works the same for us today.

The Barriers to a See-through Life - Acts 19:13-20

Barrier #1 – Pride

In Ephesus, the sons of Sceva hear about an amazing power that Paul wields. Rather than listening to the call to surrender, they begin to try and use a power which is not theirs to use. They try to cast out demons in the name of Jesus without surrendering to the power of Jesus. They want the world to look at them and see the sons of Sceva doing miraculous things – not God working through man so that the world can see Jesus.

Being see-through means getting out of the way of the power of Jesus. The sons of Sceva want to be in the spotlight. Pride pushes them to center stage. When these men hear about the miraculous things being done in the name of Jesus, they begin using the name of Jesus in order to make a name for themselves. It points directly to pride. Pride is the need to be in charge. Pride leads us to be in the center. When we occupy the center of our own lives, we push Jesus out of the way. We take control instead of surrendering. Pride in looking successful or prestigious, pride in how we are perceived by others, or pride in how we accomplish goals in our own strength does not display the power of Jesus in our lives. Pride simply displays who we are to the world. We cannot spread the good news of grace if we are focused on self. Overcoming pride means letting Jesus shine in our lives.

Barrier #2 – Clutter

The Christians in Ephesus have heard and obeyed the voice of Jesus. Observing Paul's transparency, they begin to recognize the need to allow God to be the single shining light in their lives. They began to put away the things in their lives that do not point to God.

Sorcery and magic scrolls – things that the world looks at as powerful – are burned to make room for God. As God fills them up and begins shining in their lives, the impact of transparency is seen in the community of Ephesus.

Like the Ephesians, there are things in our lives which must be destroyed in order to make room for Jesus. Bad habits, poor decisions, and harmful relationships must be set aside. Jesus calls us to offer ourselves to Him as a sacrifice. Our wills are lost in His will. Our desires are transformed to reflect His desire. Sometimes the things we must give up are painful. Jesus is the Great Physician. When we strip our hearts of the clutter in order to make room for Jesus, He takes over and heals our hurts, redirects our steps, and assumes control. He shines in our lives as a beacon for others to follow.

The Impact of a See-through Life – Acts 19:23-41

As Paul preaches in Ephesus, a great many people start to live lives surrendered to God. Their lives are so see-through that the people see Jesus shining through them. The impact on the community is staggering. So many people are listening to the voice of God that people have stopped listening to the voice of Artemis. The business of sin is no longer able to thrive. In fact, those who peddle idolatry and self-satisfaction suffer a significant loss of revenue.

Transparency shows our community how God calls His people to live. Transparency models the righteousness of God to others so that they can live the same way. When His people are living transparent lives, sin has no place to hide because the hearts of men are open to the power of God. Just imagine if Jesus shined so brightly in your community that sin wasn't profitable for businesses. What if store owners and shopping centers had to conform their wares to what people who are surrendered to Jesus would buy? In Ephesus it was a reality.

When we shine, we can impact our neighborhoods and communities in the same way.

COOL DOWN

Being See-through

Transparency allows the world to see Christ in us. As we commit to living a see-through life, we dedicate ourselves to living out Galatians 2:20 – *"I have been crucified with Christ and I no longer live, but Christ lives in me."* Jesus becomes the focus of our lives and hearts. We crucify the old man and die daily to the things that darken and cloud our transparency. We walk away from pride and burn the clutter that creates barriers to others seeing Jesus in us. As Christ lives in us, people will see Him and the transformational power of the cross working in our lives. A church that spreads is a church that is see-through.

Discussion Questions

1. Describe someone you know who lives a transparent life. What do they look like? How do you know that God lives in them?
2. Answer this question for yourself – what do people see when they look at me?
3. How does pride keep us from being transparent before the world?
4. What kinds of things to we need to let go of, burn, or destroy in order to be more transparent?
5. Read Acts 19:25-27. Is it possible to have the kind of impact on our community that the church had on the community of Ephesus? How?
6. How will being a church that is see-through help us to be a church that spreads?

Lesson 9
A Church That Shepherds
Acts 20:1-38

Key Verse:

Keep watch over yourselves and all the flock of which the Holy Spirit has made you overseers. Be shepherds of the church of God, which he bought with his own blood (Acts 20:28).

WARM UP

Some conversations just stick with you. I can vividly remember one from a long time ago. I had driven about 45 minutes to meet with a man who worked with a congregation that was steadily growing and impacting their town with the love of Jesus. Sitting in the donut shop, I asked him about his major concerns and ministry goals. Without hesitation he launched into a discussion of shepherding. He worked with a congregation that needed elders, but nobody in the congregation felt qualified to lead. "We are going to have to raise our elders up from our children." he said. That was his concern. I had never heard, or even thought about looking at leadership like this. Here was someone willing to hold up the characteristics of elders and deacons for boys in elementary school. "How do you do that?" He spoke at length about leadership coming from a surrendered life.

Teaching young men to surrender to committed marriages, study, teaching, and prayer was the only way that the church could have the leadership it needed. The church there was surrendering itself to living like shepherds so that their children could grow up with the characteristics of shepherds.

WORK OUT

The Good Shepherd

A church that spreads is a church that shepherds. Jesus is the Good Shepherd (John 10:11) and the Shepherd and Overseer of our souls (I Peter 2:25). Those who follow Jesus are people who are being trans-formed to look like Jesus. This applies to shepherding.

Shepherding is the intentional imitation of Christ toward those around us. Elders are called shepherds of God's flock and are given the responsibility for the church as a whole to live out Christ before the congregation and help others follow His example. Elders model what it means to look like Jesus to the flock that has been entrusted into their care. Elders are spiritually mature men who understand, live out, and can teach others how to live like Jesus. Their example is the example of Jesus. Every follower of Christ should surrender their lives to the qualities that an elder is meant to possess. Although we are not all called or qualified to serve as elders, we are all called to look like Jesus.

The call to walk with Jesus is the call to look like Jesus. We surrender our lives to be like Him. The elders among us are men who have lived a long time with Jesus. They have learned to pass on faith, to invite people into the journey of righteousness. They model for the church what they live in their families. A dedication to being changed by Jesus. Shouldn't we all strive for that? We all want to shine with the light of Jesus. We all want to experience transformation at His hands. We, the followers of Jesus, want to have stable marriages, faithful children, good relationships, and homes full of the presence of Christ. We all want to live in the shadow of the Good Shepherd. We all want to learn to lives as He lives. We all want to be more Christ-like, more like Him.

Christians individually hold this same responsibility to look like Jesus for the people around us. As we do this, we are going to love, encourage, teach, hold accountable, admonish, and be patient with those to whom we are connected. In this way, we are all called to shepherd and have hearts that love and care for those in God's family.

Learning to Shepherd - Acts 20:7-12

Paul is on the final leg of his Third Missionary Journey. After spending two years in Ephesus, the apostle is on his way to Jerusalem to deliver a contribution of love to the Christians there. The port city of Troas is a stop on this journey. Here Paul gathers with the Christians and spends time with them before he continues on his journey.

It is Sunday night. The Christians gather to break bread (participate in the Lord's Supper) and to hear the Word of God. As Paul preaches, a young man named Eutychus falls asleep and tumbles out of a third story window. Paul rushes down the stairs, embraces the young man, and God restores life to Eutychus.

In this snapshot, we see five powerful elements of shepherding.

1. Christians who shepherd seek out opportunities to be with other Christians.

Shepherds live among the flock. They spend their lives with the sheep. A shepherd's life is intertwined with the lives of his lambs. We cannot be the people God calls us to be in isolation. A church that shepherds begins with a group of Christians who live their lives together. They are a connected, intimate, sharing, transparent body that cares for one another and watches out for each member.

2. Christians who shepherd help others go into God's presence.

The time that Christians spend together is to have a powerful purpose and focus. Fellowship is about more than eating together and enjoying each other's company. It is primarily about opening doors to help each other move into God's presence. We must help each other have open eyes to see God's hand, open ears to hear His voice, open hands that imitate His service, and feet that follow in His footsteps. The variety of gifts and talents that He puts into a group of His people are to be used to help each other "reach unity in the faith and in the knowledge of the Son of God and become mature, attaining to the whole measure of the fullness of Christ." (Ephesians 4:13). In other words, our times together are to help us become full of Christ – to look like Jesus.

3. Christians who shepherd talk about God and the power of His grace in our lives.

As Paul preaches to the Christians in Troas and encourages the elders in Ephesus, he points them to God. He holds up the standard of truth and encourages them to live like Jesus. In Troas, his great love for them compels him to fill them with God's Word late into the night. In Ephesus, he urges the elders to hold fast to the truth that God has lifted up before them. In every place, Paul holds up the standard of Jesus and invites, urges, pleads, and encourages them to let Jesus be the one and only truth that guides their lives.

As members of God's family, we are expected to point people to Jesus. We must become a people who participate in spiritual conversations. Conversations centered around Jesus. We must learn to tell each other what God is doing in our lives. How He is transforming our days and calling us to walk a more abundant life in Him. We must be able to encourage each other with the words of Jesus. We must be so intertwined that we can hold each other accountable to the standard of the cross. Talking about Jesus with fellow Christians helps us point to Jesus in our speech with everyone we meet. We become familiar with the words of faith that point others to see Jesus at work.

4. Christians who shepherd rush to meet the needs of one who is hurting.

Tending to the wounded and helping the broken are primary functions of shepherding. The health of each individual sheep is precious to our Shepherd, and He calls us to look out for each other and walk with those who are hurting. He calls us to stop and listen to the pain-racked hearts around us, taking time to look beneath the surface and measure the ache that often echoes deep within. Jesus is compassionate, and those who look like Him are moved by a passion to help those He loves.

5. Christians who shepherd wrap another in the arms of God's love.

The picture of Paul with his arms around Eutychus is a powerful one. Equally powerful is the picture of the Ephesian elders with their arms around Paul in Acts 20:37. Touch is essential to a shepherd's care of the sheep. We are to touch one another's lives. Our society encourages isolation and "bubble living" – you stay in your space, and I'll stay in mine. When our lives touch, we have to make room for one another's hurts, worries, cares, joys, and preferences. Gentleness and genuineness remind us all that we live in God's arms. Living in that embrace, we are called us to open our arms and hearts to those around us.

COOL DOWN

Living as Shepherds

Shepherding is the gentle art of caring for another with the love of Christ. It opens the door into the presence of God and helps us walk together into the fullness of His grace. Christians with shepherding hearts see the hurts and needs of others and respond with tender mercy. Jesus tells us that love must be the defining characteristic of the people who are called by His name (John 13:34-35). It is our love for one another that will catch the attention of the world and help us become a church that spreads.

Discussion Questions

1. In what way are all of us called to individually shepherd or care for those among God's people?

2. Why is it important for our lives to be interconnected with other Christians? How does that help us "shepherd" each other?

3. Describe the actions of someone in your congregation who helps you enter God's presence and see the movement of God in your life. What have you learned from them that will help you shepherd someone else in the same way?

4. How will talking about God and holding up the standard of Jesus help you shepherd someone close to you?

5. How powerful is the impact of someone's compassion during a time of pain and hurt? How do we develop a heart that is sensitive to the needs around us?

6. How will you commit to shepherding someone this week?

7. How will being a church that shepherds help us to be a church that spreads?

Lesson 10
A Church That Shares
Acts 21:1 – 22:21

Key Verse:

You will be his witness to all men of what you have seen and heard (Acts 22:15).

WARM UP

"Therefore, whoever humbles himself like this child is the greatest in the kingdom of heaven" (Matthew 18:4)

I still marvel at the truth of these words. I was sitting in the doctor's waiting room with my three-year-old son. You have to know that he's a social little guy. He talks to everybody, which sometimes makes it hard to walk through the grocery store. You also need to know that at this stage in his life, he is completely engrossed with Thomas, the Tank Engine. Not feeling well, my son, Thomas the train, and I were all waiting to see the doctor. A few minutes after our arrival, another little boy came in and started playing at the little table provided for children. My social son saw an opportunity to make a friend, and off he went. The two sat at the little table and my son gave him Thomas.

They played for a while, laughing and running over each other. It was a grand time. The nurse came out, called our name, and we got ready to go. My son got up, said "bye," and started to follow the nurse. He left Thomas with the other little boy. At the same time, the dad of the little boy and I both reached out to get Thomas and return him. My son took the train and went back to the table to leave him with his new friend. In that moment, I was just as proud as I could be. Not because he learned something from me, but because in that moment I saw how he looks like Jesus.

Children do that. They share. Without reservation, without thought to cost or personal gain, they share. I know, I know. Not all children share so readily. And sharing becomes harder as we mature. But that just makes the lesson more important to learn. Sharing is a Christ-like quality that helps us surrender to the power of Jesus in our lives.

WORK OUT

Sharing Our Resources – Acts 21:1-16

As Paul journeys toward Jerusalem, his mission is a mission of sharing. Examining his past travel and his letters to the churches in Rome and Corinth, we see that Paul is taking a gift to Jerusalem to help out the poor saints of that city. Paul is strengthening the bonds between brothers and opening lines of communication between Christians. Follow Paul as we see his plan to go to Jerusalem:

- ***Acts 19:21-22*** – In Ephesus, Paul makes a plan to travel to Jerusalem. His travels will first include stops in Macedonia and Achaia.
- ***Romans 15:25-26*** – Paul shares his intent to travel to Jerusalem

in his letter to the Romans. Here he mentions the gift that those in Macedonia and Achaia have put together to send to Jerusalem.

- **I Corinthians 16:1-4** – Paul gives the church instructions on taking up the collection for the poor saints in Jerusalem.
- **Acts 21:1-16** – As Paul moves through this region, he is intent on taking the gift from the Asian churches to the church in Jerusalem. The Spirit has moved in Paul, warning him that the journey will be a difficult one ending in imprisonment. But Paul never wavers. He is intent on sharing a gift with his brethren in Jerusalem.

Sharing Our Burdens - Acts 21:17-40

As Paul enters Jerusalem he is greeted warmly by the church there, but at the same time there is a problem. Paul's preaching among the Gentiles has stirred some questions in the hearts of Jerusalem Christians. There is some concern about how Paul will be received by the Jewish Christians. The Christians in Jerusalem still hold zealously to the Law, while Paul works among the Gentiles and preaches that all men are free to follow Christ alone. As Paul seeks to connect with the church in Jerusalem, he joins with four men who have taken a vow. Paul shares their burden. He knows that though he is not bound by the Law, sharing in the vow will ease tensions among the Jerusalem brothers. By sharing their burden, he reaffirms the connection that exists between the Gentile and Jewish churches.

Being a church that shares means walking with each other through the problems of life. People struggle in this fallen world. We struggle with sin, with family problems, with financial difficulties, or health issues. You name it and someone in your church, or someone in your home, has struggled with it. The church is not a place to hide our hurts. It is a place to walk alongside each other and share the burden. Ecclesiastes 4:9 tells us, *"Two are better than one…"* We walk together to share what is on our hearts. To lift up each other. To stand firm for Jesus. We walk together and share our burdens so that we can look more like Jesus who carries our burdens.

Sharing the Story of Jesus - Acts 22:1-21

As Paul shares the burden of the vow, he is recognized by some Jews from Asia. They stir the crowds up against Paul, and Paul is arrested. Paul uses this opportunity to once again share with those around him. This time he shares the message of Jesus.

Often sharing the message of Jesus seems intimidating. We know how to share our resources. We are willing to share a burden. But what message does Jesus want us to share with those around us? Paul gives us the answer as he shares the story of Jesus.

Paul shares the story of who he was before he knew Jesus. Acts 22:1-5

Paul had been a persecutor of Christians. He had attacked the body of Christ. His zeal was great. His mission was clear. But Paul was wrong in what he did. By attacking the church, Paul set himself against Jesus.

There was a time when we, too, were fighting Jesus. A time when we lived in sin, without any desire to be changed. But like Paul, God will not leave us in a place of sin. He pursues us with passion, seeking to share a relationship with us. As we share the message of the cross with those around us, we must be honest about the fact that we were once sinners and opposed to God. We must tell the world that Jesus calls all men to be His.

**Paul shares the transforming experience of meeting Jesus.
Acts 22:6-13**

It is a powerful moment. It is THE road to Damascus experience. But no matter who you are, the experience is the same. Like Paul, there came a day when you met Jesus and faced the fact that you needed a relationship with Him. It is a moment when you cried out to be changed. Like Paul, we need to be changed in action, attitude, and focus. Sharing the message of Jesus means talking about how God is moving in our lives and how God is transforming us day by day and minute by minute.

Paul shares the call to surrender to a lifetime of walking with Jesus. Acts 22:14-21

As Paul rises from the waters of baptism, his life is changed. He no longer lives in his own will, but is commissioned to tell all men what he has seen and heard. It is a moment when the entire course of his life is redirected and transformed.

Take a moment to walk through the three elements of Paul's story. Use his outline to walk through the pieces of your own story. Think about who you were before you knew Jesus. Remember the experience of meeting Jesus and becoming His. Impress on your mind the way God calls you to walk with Him today.

COOL DOWN

A Church that Shares

From childhood, sharing is a quality that we value in others. We teach our children to share. We develop friendships with those who are willing to share their lives with us. Sharing both leads to and flows from connection. When people share, they invest their resources, time, emotions, and selves in another. Sharing helps to build community and open doors of communication. The act of sharing is an act of transformation. When we share, we imitate Christ who shared Himself completely with us. Sharing our resources reflects the heart of One who gives us more than we can ask or imagine. Sharing our burdens points the way to One who invites the weary and heavy-laden to His side. Sharing our story opens the door for God to shower grace on hurting hearts and broken lives. A church that spreads is a church that shares.

Discussion Questions

1. What kinds of things are we called to share with the world around us?
2. How does sharing our resources help us to lift up Jesus?
3. How does sharing someone's burdens help us to lift up Jesus?
4. In what way is sharing your story of Jesus difficult or intimidating?
5. Who can you tell your story to this week? How will you do it?
6. How will being a church that shares help us to be a church that spreads?

Lesson 11
A Church That Stands
Acts 22:30 – 24:27

Key Verse:

The following night the Lord stood near Paul and said, "Take courage! As you have testified about me in Jerusalem, so you must also testify in Rome (Acts 23:11).

WARM UP

Think for just a minute about some of the places we visit or shop. When you think of McDonalds' your mind immediately goes to hamburgers. Baskin-Robbins® is known for great ice cream. Hewlett-Packard® makes computers. Starbucks is where you get coffee. Each of these places is known for one thing. They have an easily recognized identity. They have invested huge amounts of resources so that consumers will identify them with one thing.

Though the church is not a business, the church should have an easily recognized core. The church should be immediately identified with Jesus. The church is defined by who we stand by and who stands by us. Being a church that stands means first and foremost recognizing that Jesus stands by His people. The people He calls, He empowers. The people He leads, He transforms. As the people of Jesus, we are identified as His body. We stand with and in Him in every moment. We shine as lights to the world around us so that all can see Jesus. Transformation and power flow from the relationship that exists between Jesus and His people.

As we walk with Paul, we can see how Jesus stands in relationship with Paul and how that relationship fuels Paul's drive to shine for Jesus. That same relationship is what defines a church that stands today.

WORK OUT

Where We Stand – Acts 22:30 - 24:27

We stand in a relationship powered by the resurrection. Acts 22:30-23:20

Forewarned by the Holy Spirit, Paul now stands as a prisoner in Jerusalem. The accusations of the Jews have reached a fevered pitch and Paul must now go before them to answer for his actions. Just as Paul always does, he rests firmly in his relationship with God as he stands before the Sanhedrin. Here is a group of 70 men who in many ways rule the Jewish people. They are often thought of as a court of men whose task is to judge. But more than that, these men are called to raise up the standard of God's law. They are to show the world what it means to live in relationship with the Lord and prepare God's people for the coming Messiah. Standing before these men, Paul recognizes the one truth they most need to embrace. Paul points them to the cross and the empty tomb. He knows that one thing must be firmly in the forefront for anyone who would follow Jesus – the resurrection. No other event is more central to having a relationship with Jesus. The resurrection shows us the ultimate power of God to forgive sin and bring the dead to a new life in Christ. Paul's aim is not simply to confound these men. Paul's aim is to bring to light the central truth that God pursues man and has built a bridge to Himself through the blood of Christ.

That same message is central to our walk with Jesus. The resurrection is the event which shows us God's unending love for man. The resurrection shows us the hope of life after death – both the physical death that all mortals must face, but also the death that comes from a life lived outside of relationship with God. Those who surrender to the power of the resurrection no longer face the death of sin. They live in the strength of God's provision today. There is forgiveness in the hands of God. There is a power that God freely extends to His people. There is a strength that comes from experiencing the passion that God has for man.

We stand in a relationship defined by the reality of God's presence. Acts 23:11-22

As the Sanhedrin argues over the power of the resurrection, Paul is spirited away to safety. The next evening the Lord has a message for Paul. God comes near, standing with Paul to encourage him and give him strength. It is a strength that Paul will need in the days to come. As the Jews plot to take his life, Paul must rest in the knowledge that God is near. God is in charge. God can move men and events to accomplish His will.

Too often, we look at the world around us and despair over the lack of control we have to change men and events. God wants us to rest in Him, recognizing that we have no power apart from Him. God's movement is the only power capable of changing the world. As we stand in the world God wants us to look beyond men and situations and focus clearly on His presence. God is not far from us. He walks closely with His people in the world to effect transformation. His call is clearly heard in the lives of His people. His movement is seen when we have eyes focused on Him.

Learning to rest in God's presence is a deliberate act. Just as David stood before Saul and remembered the death of a lion and bear (I Samuel 17:34), we must take time to look into our own history and see how God has moved. Seeing God in our past helps us rest in His presence. Another way we can learn to rest in the presence of God is to rehearse God's presence in the world around us. Over and over in the Psalms, writers point to deer, the stars, pastures, trees, and people as reminders of God's work in our world. Seeing God in our front yard, our church, and our families reminds us that God is still present in our lives today. Learning to rest in God's presence means rehearsing God's presence. Like a singer learning a song or an actor learning a part, we must tell ourselves over and over what God has done and how God is moving.

We stand in a relationship which call us to raise His standard before the world. Acts 24:1-27

As Paul's life is threatened, God moves Paul to Caesarea, giving Paul the opportunity to stand before Felix the governor. Paul again shows us what it means to be a church that stands. Every part of Paul's dealings with Felix becomes a moment for Paul to raise the standard of Jesus. Paul never wavers. He knows that Christians are called to lift up one thing – Jesus. Paul shows Felix how Jesus has changed every part of His life. Paul talks about lifting up Jesus before the Gentiles and the Jews alike. Paul speaks with passion about the impact of following Jesus. Felix listens but makes no immediate moves. In fact, Paul is left to deal with Felix for two years. But Paul is persistent. Paul continues to lift up Jesus day after day, encounter after encounter.

Like Paul, we who share a relationship with Jesus are called to raise one standard before the world. We are called to lift up Jesus. The transformation that we experience in a relationship with Him fuels a passion to talk about Him. His great love for us gives us the strength to raise Him as the only standard for the world day after day and encounter after encounter.

Think about all of the opportunities that you will get to lift up the standard of Jesus today. You will be given an opportunity to lift up the standard of His love in your family and among your friends as you interact with those who are close to your heart. You will get a chance to lift up the standard of His integrity as you go to work or to the grocery store today. Those you come into contact with will have a chance to see Jesus today because of the places you walk. The post office, the gas station, and the bank all become places to stand with God and to lift up Jesus in your life. We live a life of unending opportunities to spread the grace and mercy of Jesus.

COOL DOWN

Standing for Jesus

A church that spreads is a church that stands for one thing – Jesus Christ. His name gives us identity. His death gives us new life. His love gives us purpose. His grace gives us hope. His power gives us courage. His words give us direction. The relationship that the church shares with Christ is empowered by the resurrection and defined by the presence of God. Christians are called to raise one standard and speak one name. God stands by us. When we become a church that stands firmly in Him, we become a people who can spread His name for His glory.

Discussion Questions

1. How does the resurrection open our eyes to the fact that Jesus stands with His people?
2. How does the resurrection help us to stand as lights in the world?
3. How do we learn to confidently rest in the truth that God stands with His people?
4. How does God's presence help us to stand as lights in the world?
5. How does God's standard show us that He stands with us?
6. How will you be extra aware this week that God stands by you?
7. How will you be extra focused this week on standing by God?
8. How will being a church that stands help us to be a church that spreads?

Lesson 12
A Church That Sets An Example
Acts 25:1 – 26:32

Key Verse:

Paul replied, "Short time or long—I pray God that not only you but all who are listening to me today may become what I am, except for these chains" **(Acts 26:29).**

WARM UP

Best known for his *Farmer's Almanac*, Ben Franklin knew the power of example. In the 1750s, Pennsylvania farmers were having a tough time growing grain. Benjamin Franklin experimented with different things and eventually discovered that Plaster of Paris is useful for fertilizing growing grain. Upon making the discovery, Franklin shared this information with all of his neighbors and friends. They would not believe him. In fact, the Pennsylvania farmers dismissed Franklin's suggestion and continued to try and grow their grain in the same old ways. Franklin, on the other hand, while planting his fields, wrote in large letters, "This Has Been Plastered." He then filled the words with Plaster of Paris and sowed his seed. Over the next few weeks as the grain grew, the words became more and more pronounced. The plaster worked. Franklin's words were greener than the grain growing around them. As farmers stopped to look, the letters stood out and everyone knew that Franklin had discovered how to encourage grain to grow in Pennsylvania. His example spoke louder than his words.[1]

Having learned from his own experience, Franklin decided that he wanted street lights in the city of Philadelphia. So, "he hung a beautiful lantern on a long bracket before his own door. Then he kept the glass brightly polished, and carefully and religiously lit the wick every evening at the approach of dusk. It wasn't long before Franklin's neighbors began placing lights in brackets before their homes, and soon the entire city awoke to the value of street lighting and took up the matter with interest and enthusiasm."[2]

We all know the power of an example. Examples help bring a fact or truth into three dimensions. An abstract concept or idea may be difficult to get our minds around, but an example helps to make the abstract concrete – easier to see and understand. Examples help to make truth accessible and personal. A church that spreads is a church that sets an example.

1   Parton, James. The Life and Times of Benjamin Franklin: Volume 1. Mason Brothers Publishing. New York. 1864. Page 313

2   Tan, P. L. (1996). Encyclopedia of 7700 illustrations : A treasury of illustrations, anecdotes, facts and quotations for pastors, teachers and Christian workers. Garland TX: Bible Communications.

WORK OUT

Paul's Example – Acts 25:1-22

Paul offered his very life as an example of what it means to be Christ's. *"Follow my example as I follow the example of Christ."* (I Corinthians 11:1). We often read Paul's words and put them on a pedestal as something that only apostles are called to do. Paul's words are a reflection, however, of the way that God means for all Christians to live in the world. Our example – the way we look, act, move, speak, serve, obey, and love like Jesus – brings the truth about Christ into three dimensions for those around us. When they can see the power of the gospel working in our lives, it opens the door to the idea that God can work in their lives as well.

Paul shows us how to live as an example at a tough time in his life. The robust, traveling preacher spends two years in confinement. During this time, Festus replaces Felix as the Roman Governor of the region. As soon as the new governor takes office, the Jews again bring charges against Paul, petitioning Festus to bring Paul to Jerusalem where they plan to ambush and kill him. Festus commands the Jews to present their evidence in Caesarea, and we see the hand of God once again protect Paul.

It becomes evident to Paul that Festus' interest lies in placating the Jews in the region rather than in the justice due to one man. Having already spent two years in prison while Felix waited for a bribe, Paul's hope of a rapid resolution to his legal situation evaporates as Festus seeks favor with the Jews. Recognizing that unless he acts he will likely stay in prison or be handed over to the Jews in Jerusalem, Paul appeals to Caesar. His time in prison is not wasted. He sets an example for the leaders he encounters.

Paul's example before Festus – A Centered Focus - Acts 25:18-19

As Festus explains Paul's legal situation to King Agrippa, the impact of Paul's example comes shining through. Paul's example begins with *a centered focus*. Paul didn't get caught up in the arguments and issues that Festus normally sees. His arrest and continued imprisonment center on Paul's conviction concerning the resurrection of Jesus.

While Festus believes that Paul is caught up in a petty squabble with his fellow Jews over the life or death of Jesus, Paul remains centered on the power of the resurrection.

The church's example must be cemented in our focus on the resurrection of Jesus. There are many issues raging in our society that call for our attention and compete for our focus. It is important that we center our lives around the cross. The resurrection must define who we are as the church. The cross must leave a deep imprint on our hearts. In a fragmented world, a centered focus is a powerful example of the work of God in our lives.

Paul's example before Agrippa – A Changed Purpose - Acts 25:23-26:23

As Paul stands before Agrippa, he spends his time describing himself as a man of changed purpose. Before he met Jesus on the road to Damascus, he was committed to the destruction of the church and to opposing the name of Jesus. After his encounter with the Lord on the road to Damascus, **he has a new purpose**. God appoints him as a servant and a witness. His new purpose is found in the new relationship he now shares with Christ. He is to tell others about the power God has to change every heart.

Our purpose flows from Jesus. From the very moments of His birth in Bethlehem, Christ's presence called the world to see God. Angels sang at His birth to announce the presence of God in the world. From the moment we give ourselves to Jesus in the waters of baptism, we take on the purpose of pointing to Jesus. The world around us needs to see a living example of God's movement. Walking the roads of Judea and the streets of Jerusalem and Jericho, Jesus talked about what it means to walk with God. The church today must live with the purpose of showing people how to walk in a relationship with Jesus. Our lips need to be full of His praise. Our lives must be full of His mercy. Our thoughts must be full of His beauty. Our days must be full of His presence. We must deliberately take steps to let Jesus shine in our lives.

In John 4:14, Jesus tells a Samaritan woman, *"Indeed, the water I give him will become in him a spring of water welling up to eternal life."* In these words of Jesus, we have a picture of overflow. Being full of Jesus means we overflow into the lives of those around us. When we are full of His purpose, we share that purpose with others. Jesus came to call men into relationship with God. We do the same.

Paul's example before Agrippa – A Call to Relationship - Acts 26:24-32

Wrapping up his defense before Festus and Agrippa, Paul asks Agrippa a simple question – do you believe in the prophets? **It is a call to relationship.** It is a loaded question because in the question is a compelling call to walk closely with God. It is interesting that Agrippa understands two important things about the prophets. First, he knows that the central message of the prophets is a call to walk in relationship with God. The prophets urge people to recognize that God is close and wants their whole hearts. Second, Agrippa seems to understand that the prophets point to Jesus. If he says he believes the message of the prophets, he understands that he is surrendering to the call of the prophets to believe in the One God sent.

The church carries a similar message to the world. God loves all men. He longs for each person to be His. Jesus is the answer to man's deepest need. As Christians set an example before the world, their example is an invitation – come walk with God. Be His. Surrender to the lordship of Jesus Christ. It is a call to relationship that is made compelling to the world around us because we move as living examples of what it means to belong to God.

Setting An Example

And so the question comes, "How does your example invite people to share a relationship with Jesus?" What message is growing in the field of your life? People need to see the words of Jesus written clearly in how you live. How do you encourage others to join with the light? Living an example means we surrender every moment to the love of Jesus. Every word, every action must be an example that points to Him.

Discussion Questions

1. Why is a centered focus important to our example?
2. How does Paul explain his purpose as he describes his life before Christ? How does he describe his purpose after he met Jesus?
3. In what way do all Christians share the purpose Christ outlined for Paul in Acts 26:16-18?
4. How does living out our purpose in Christ help us set an example for those around us?
5. How does your life serve as a call to a relationship with Jesus for those you meet?
6. How will being a church that sets an example help us to be a church that spreads?

Lesson 13
A Church That Spans The Globe
Acts 27:1 – 28:31

Key Verse:

Boldly and without hindrance he preached the kingdom of God and taught about the Lord Jesus Christ **(Acts 28:31).**

WARM UP

Over and over as we have walked with Paul through the second half of the book of Acts, we notice one theme rises above all else. A church that spreads does so because Christians are focused on Jesus. A focus on Jesus broadens our horizons, sharpens our vision, and fires our passion. We see through the eyes of God when we focus on Jesus.

John 3:16 tells us that God so loved *the world*. Not just one group of people. Not just one city or country. God's love extends to every individual who walks the face of the earth. God's love is a love that spans the globe.

Because of this great love, Jesus went to the cross so that *whoever* believes in Him would have eternal life. Look at that whoever. Anyone and everyone who surrenders their lives to Jesus can walk with Him from today through eternity. It doesn't matter where you come from or where you have been. It doesn't matter where you live – in the city, in the country, in the woods, or in the deserts. People from the United States, Canada, Brazil, Ukraine, South Africa, and all over the world have access to a relationship with Jesus through the power of the cross.

God's vision, grace, and call reach into every part of our world. God's desire spans the globe. When we walk with Jesus, our horizons are stretched beyond our understanding. A church that spreads is a church that spans the globe.

WORK OUT

A Church that Spans the Globe Trusts God's Promises – Acts 27:1-44

The last two chapters of Acts give us a picture of what empowers a church to span the globe with the love of Christ, the beauty of the gospel, the call of God to all men, and the transforming power of the cross.

In Acts 27:1-44, we see a harrowing account of a shipwreck that nearly claims the life of Paul and his companions. Paul is under Roman guard and is being transported to Rome for trial before Caesar. It is late in the sailing season and a ferocious storm comes up on the Mediterranean Sea. After many days of being tossed by the waves and peering helplessly into storm-blackened skies, the crew and passengers give up hope that they will survive the storm. As discouragement floods their hearts, Paul calls the men to put their eyes and hope on God.

A church that spans the globe trusts in God's promises. Our faith is firmly rooted in the faithfulness of our God. His promises allow us to move with confidence and purpose in our world as we call people to be His. The world may rage and the storms may threaten but we know that God is in control and that when we stand with Him, the victory is sure. That confidence and surety is a beacon into the world that has given up hope.

A Church that Spans the Globe Expects God to Move – Acts 28:1-10

As Paul reaches the safety of land, he meets a group of islanders who show great kindness to the shipwrecked men washed up on shore. The warmth of a fire and the welcome of a smile give us an insight into the hearts of these people. Paul pitches in to help and a terrible thing happens. A snake attacks. The islanders know the result. Paul will die. They assume he is being divinely punished. They reason that he cannot escape a punishment for sin, be it the punishment of drowning at sea or being bitten by a deadly viper.

As Paul shakes the snake off into the flames, we see God moving. No swelling, no ill effects, and no sudden death accompany the snake bite. God intervenes to save Paul. The islanders change their mind about who Paul is. Rather than someone being punished, they see Paul as a god. Paul sees God moving to open their hearts to hear about the real God who is present. Publius, a public official, welcomes Paul into his home. Here we see God moving to heal hurts. The sick are healed, and Paul is able to point them to Jesus.

Christians move in the world with the expectation that God is at work among them. They have eyes to see His hand and hearts that respond to the way He moves among them. Whether Paul is standing before kings, talking to women by a river, or stranded on an island,

Paul expects God to move and call people to Himself. The church to-day needs to live with that same expectation. God is living and moving and active in our world. It should come as no surprise to His people that He moves on their behalf. A church that spans the globe is a church that can show people how God is moving in their lives today.

A Church that Spans the Globe Walks Together – Acts 28:11-16

As Paul travels toward Rome, he does not walk alone. Christians from Rome meet him along the way and bring comfort and joy to his journey. A church that spans the globe walks together. We recognize the power of linking hearts and hands and walking together as we move in the world as God's people.

One of the elders where I serve always prays for those around the world who are worshiping on the Lord's Day. I always have to stop and try to picture that. On the first day of the week, as our congregation gathers to worship, there are people driving in from Nebraska farms, the suburbs of Chicago, and the Black Hills of South Dakota to their local churches in order to worship. We are joined by bonds of faith. But more than that there are people on the same day who are worshiping in New York, Washington, and everyplace in between. There are villagers in Papua, New Guinea who meet in pavilions to worship. There are open air congregations in South Africa. The family of God gathers by rivers, on mountains, and near the ocean. The people of God span the globe. God's children share common purpose and common habits. Our family resemblance is incredible. We look like Jesus. I love the reminder that this is true.

This is the kind of family Paul encounters as he enters Rome. He meets a family who embraces him as one of their own. They are a family committed to praying for those outside their own little circle.

As a church that spans the globe, we need to recognize and honor this global sense of family. We can embrace a sense of global community as we walk together with Jesus.

A Church that Spans the Globe Boldly Proclaims Christ to the World - Acts 28:30-31

Paul arrives in Rome and is put under house arrest. For two years, he waits on God's timing and the moment when he will stand before Caesar and make his defense. This is not idle time for Paul. It is during these years that he writes the prison epistles (Philemon, Colossians, Ephesians, and Philippians). He also uses every opportunity to lift up the name of Jesus, proclaiming the gospel to everyone he meets.

A church that spans the globe must be a church that consistently, passionately, openly, boldly, and uncompromisingly lifts up Jesus before the world. We have one story to tell, one message to give, and one invitation to offer – Jesus. We can proclaim His name boldly because we trust in God's promises, because we fully expect God to move among us, and because we walk together on this journey of faith. The church will only spread when we root ourselves in the shadow of the cross and point people to Jesus and nothing but Jesus. There He promises that when we lift Him up, He will draw all men unto Himself.

COOL DOWN

A Church That Spreads

If there is one lesson that we take away from a study of Acts, it is this: When Jesus is lifted up, people are drawn to Him. A church that spreads is intent on lifting up Jesus. You and I as individuals must learn to lift up Jesus in our families, in our speech, in our relationships, and in our churches. Our churches must lift up Jesus in study, worship, message, and mission. It is vital that those of us who live lives surrendered to Jesus share His story with the world around us. In sharing that good news, Christ's church will spread around the world.

Discussion Questions

1. What promises has God made to you? To the church? How do these promises help us face life's difficult storms?
2. How will those promises help us be confident as we seek to be a church that spans the globe?
3. What opportunities do we have to tell people how God is moving among us?
4. How will being a church that walks together help us to be a church that spans the globe?
5. In what way should the words of Acts 28:31 be a description of our congregations?
6. What are the defining characteristics of a church that spreads?